1

Project Studies of America

By

Thomas Kielbasinski

Table of Contents

Chapter 1- Belle Vernon Evacuation Project   **4**

Homeland Security   **4**

Objective   **6**

Data Sharing   **7**

3

Emergencies and Disasters (CERT Program)   8

Emergencies and Disasters (Terrorism)   9

Preparing for Building Explosions and Bomb Threats 10

Biological   11

Nuclear and Radioactivity Threats /Protective Measures 12

Belle Vernon Evacuation Plan   13

History of Belle Vernon   17

History of North Belle Vernon   18

Current Conditions in Belle Vernon   20

Economic Development   21

Business Located in Belle Vernon   23

Churches in Belle Vernon   25

Hospitals & Airports   27

Belle Vernon Schools/Libraries   28

Radio and TV Stations   30

Housing   34

Housing type   37

Role of Professional Planner/Conclusion   38

Chapter 2- Urban Planning of Somerset County   39

Introduction   39

History of Somerset County   40

Local Areas and Attractions of Somerset County   44

Urban Development of Somerset County of Transportation   47

Enviromapper analysis of Somerset County   49

County Elected Officials of Somerset County Ideas   50

Somerset County Planning Facts   51

Chapter 2- Conclusion   53

Chapter 3-Oklahoma City NBA Expansion Stadium Project   54

Introduction/Literature on Stadium   54

Summary and Opinion of Stadium Management   56

Strengths of Expansion and Setup New Stadium   67

Chapter 3- Conclusion   69

Chapter 4- Washington and Alleghany County Planning Studies   70

Problems in Alleghany and Washington County   70

Whiskey Rebellion   **71**

National Road   **72**

Summary of Solutions to Problems   **75**

Chapter 4- Conclusion   **77**

Chapter 5- Natural Resource Conservation Services   **78**

References

Chapter 1

Belle Vernon Evacuation Project

Homeland Security

The purpose of this project is to develop a detailed plan for Belle Vernon Homeland Security is coherent and comprehensive to the authorities, which will then be implemented to make the most effective homeland security plan. This plan will focus on different areas of the town to achieve this purpose effectively.

When researching this subject matter it is essential to be aware of terms parallel to this matter. Homeland is known as where in which people live and is made up of physical geography, natural resources geography, cultural geography, social geography, and economic geography. Security is defined as the safety of the local, state, and national communities, citizens, and governments. The definition of risk assessment and planning are estimating and analyzing certain disasters of the specific location. This assessment and plan determines where an area like Belle Vernon should go with its evacuation process. The definition of mitigation is to reduce the probability of a disaster. Chief of Belle Vernon Police, John Hartman, is the officer responsible for training the residents in Belle Vernon, to be aware of what could happen even in a small area. Even though the chances are very slim of any type of an attack on an area the size of Belle Vernon or North Belle Vernon, these training and lookout efforts help make responses faster and recovery less costly. As long as it is a disaster that is within our area of control, the area can handle it, but if not the problems could affect more than just the Belle Vernon area.

Preparedness is to be alert and think ahead about areas like Belle Vernon through any type of small disasters and even larger disasters, should they occur. This also puts the federal, state and local governments into action to be better organized for the disaster in smaller areas.

The definition of response is to react to the disaster as soon as possible and is able to relief to the disaster. Response also includes the area in which relief would be provided, response for emergencies and disasters, search and rescue squads for floods, emergency shelters (Schools, and Fire Halls), medical care for the injured, hospitals if possible to reach them, the Red Cross, the Salvation Army, and mass feeding.

Recovery is the ability to return to a level of normality in a given period. The recovery of a town or city depends on the amount of damage, which may be either short term or long term. The short-term process would be for disasters such as blizzards, floods, and minor tornadoes. The short-term processes would consist of keeping food and water well stocked, candles, flashlights, and other sources of power in case the power goes out. The long-term recovery would consist of periods of months or years for recovery. After a dead hit by Hurricane Andrew in 1992 in South Florida, it took at least two years to recover. Many citizens can say that the two worst days of their life was after the Salisbury Tornadoes of May 31st and June 2nd, 1998. The clean up and recovery from these two tornadoes would take them almost a year and a half to recover from such devastation of two F-3 tornadoes. These two disasters could not be avoided because of "mother nature." If this happens to a small town like Belle Vernon, the most prepared citizens and planners cannot avoid the horrible results. This is why Homeland Security of natural disasters or terrorist problems through evacuation processes has to be well thought out and planned.

Objective

Maps of Belle Vernon will be created to develop a coherent evacuation plan for this area. These maps will highlight major highways, hospitals, doctor's offices, schools, police stations, and fire departments. These highways and byways will be used to set up a number of routes. One route may be used for emergency vehicles that will be responding to the emergency, and other routes will be used to evacuate the community out of the Belle Vernon area. All hospitals, fire stations, police stations and doctor's office will be identified.

Each area will be examined and assessed in order to make sure that the locations identified are easily accessible for emergency vehicles and the community, so that an evacuation may take place in timely and organized manner. Having knowledge of the location of other elements such as water, sewer and power lines are essential in emergency situations.

All medical facilities in the area will need to be assessed so that each facility can be used for the variety of medical needs. In addition, all medical supplies will need to be

counted. A plan of how to distribute all supplies will need to be developed to ensure that each medical and shelter receives the correct amount of supplies.

Another area that will need to be addressed when considering possible terrorist attacks is the use of the bridges and the waterways. Secondly, there will need to be checkpoints in place.

Data Sharing

Data sharing is important because to come up with the best plan for the town of Belle Vernon, experts and other major figures will help provide some data for Fayette and Washington Counties and not just the town of Belle Vernon, and North Belle Vernon. This plan must contain good facilities, maintenance in planning and information on every aspect of the town. The dependability of the Internet for of information is critical because not all of the information on the Internet is accurate.

The cost of GIS data sharing varies from place to place. Over 90 percent of Homeland Security data is the total cost of GIS in itself. This cost easily runs into the billions and billions of dollars from the mining industry and large municipalities. With Belle Vernon being so small the cost would be outrageous.

Emergencies and Disasters (CERT Program)

In Homeland Security of Pennsylvania, there is a program that would greatly benefit the small community of Belle Vernon. This program is called Community Emergency Response Team or CERT. CERT was developed in Los Angeles, CA by the Los Angeles Fire Department in 1985. These CERT programs have been developed in 45 states and 340 communities, which shows that the idea is spreading.

There is a training program for Belle Vernon citizens, if interested for 20 hours during a 7 day week period. These meetings cover fire disasters, medical rescue purposes and body of water rescues. This program is being to be further developed and implemented with over 400,000 volunteers in 56 states and countries throughout the world.

Emergencies and Disasters (Terrorism)

The definition of Terrorism is violent acts against a nation, country, and state that include intimidation and ransom. These terrorist or evil organizations make people of their government feel hopeless and worthless to fight against these acts.

The threats of violence are very slim for a community like Belle Vernon but the Chief of Police in Belle Vernon has tried to make citizens aware of the different threats of terrorism, which include: assassinations, kidnappings, hijackings, bomb scares, and cyber attacks. The training program involved with Chief John Hartman includes the threatening of any of these actions in the Belle Vernon area. For example, the chief of police got a complaint of us college students taking pictures of bridges, buildings, infrastructures, and complexes. This was a major concern in a small community because since 9-11 everyone has been on high alert even in the smaller areas of the country.

Some of the issues that Chief John Hartman keeps his community aware of are: always be aware of the communities surroundings, report all suspicious activity, always to evacuate the closest emergency exit in buildings, and keep first aid a kit handy for medical treatment in your home and on your job, for yourself and others.

There is also a different type of terrorism called cyber attacks. These cyber attacks can happen in three different ways: through wires, phone lines, and party access systems. These cyber attacks can affect the following: ATM machines, computer data, intercept telephone call conversations, and trusted party access system. There is a general evacuation method through homeless shelters when harmful materials are released in restricted areas.

Preparing and Responding in Building Explosions

The proper methods to prepare and respond are to review evacuation emergency methods and know your direction around your place of work or apartment you rent. Another factor is to know where emergency equipment is, in case of a small fire in hallways or down stairs or in offices. Secondly, then get CPR training or first aid education just in case someone is in need of immediate help. The following things are a must for owners of buildings and complexes: portable batteries, flashlights, first aid equipment, and specialized tape to mark dangerous zones and locations.

Bomb Threats

For people of Belle Vernon, if you receive a bomb threat get as much information as possible from the bomber as quickly as possible and report it to the police. Be very aware of the follow things: unfamiliar packages, letters and gifts sent to you because they could be bomb type devices.

Biological

The following are specific biological dangers that could cause viruses and diseases through any type of unfamiliar bacteria, viruses, and toxins. The causes of many deaths are through air pollution. Some other dangers are spread through animals and insects such as mice, flies, and mosquitoes. Because some chemicals are sprayed over vegetables and certain types of feeds are given to cattle; food and water contamination can be avoided by making sure that all food is cooked to the maximum and that all meat is cooked till completely done. An example of biological terrorist attacks happened in the fall of 2001, when Anthrax was sent to different government offices and agencies through the mail. This deadly white powder disrupted the mail and other important activities.

A major reason to make people more aware of terrorist threats in certain areas is so the nation as a whole can be more prepared if something like 9-11 should happen again. This is also making smaller communities aware that it doesn't necessarily have to hit the bigger cities for it to be a major disaster. The country also wants its citizens to feel as safe and secure as they were before 9-11.

When in comes to decontamination, there are some things that you should do way to make sure that you don't become contaminated or contaminate someone else. Keep these following things in mind when worried about contamination: Remove all possible contaminated clothing, flush eyes out with non contaminated water, wash and rinse face with soap and water, and go to the closest hospital for medical checkup.

Nuclear and Radioactivity Threats

The Nuclear bomb has only been used by the United States against Japan in August of 1945 twice. There have been threats by U.S., Russia, and Iraq from the Cold War Era 1945-1990 and Gulf War Era 1991-1992, but none of these threats have been followed through because the nuclear bomb is 100 times dangerous than a grenade. The Radioactive bomb or "dirty bomb" is more likely to be used in attacks in terrorism because they are easier and less expensive to get. There are several potential targets that terrorists aim for: missile bases, federal government locations, subways, bus stations, manufacturing businesses, and other important businesses. These are also potential targets for Belle Vernon residents, citizens and planners to watch out for, so this is why Chief John Hartman teaches and trains his citizens and fellow officers of the community 24/7. Without the training this will not save lives if it were to happen into community of Belle Vernon. The three keys of protection are shielding, distance and time. The shielding method is good because the thicker in material of the facility you evacuate to the better. This would include: bricklayer buildings and steel structures. The distance method is better in places like bathrooms, basements and offices where you are more likely to evacuate to a safer place. Time is the most critical because you need to evacuate to a safe location as quickly as possible.

Protective Measures and Threats

There is always a possibility of terrorist's attacks and violence. There are several different conditions or levels of terrorists' attacks. These conditions are low, elevated, guarded and severe. The government goes through proper measures to make sure everyone involved gets the feel for the Homeland Security Advisory System and well prepared protective measures for the possibility of raising the terrorism threat.

Belle Vernon/North Belle Vernon Emergency Evacuation Plan:

The purpose of this Evacuation Plan is to develop a plan for the boroughs of Belle Vernon and North Belle Vernon so that during a time of disaster the residents, workers, and community members can be evacuated in an organized manner to maintain the highest level of safety. The map indicates that there are two areas, one of these areas will be Belle Vernon and the other will be North Belle Vernon. The following guidelines and evacuation routes are to be followed in a time of disaster.

Primary Evacuation Zone: The Primary Evacuation Zone is the area that the citizens of the Belle Vernon and North Belle Vernon boroughs would be evacuated to in the event of a terrorist attack. The Primary Evacuation Zone would be in effect if Belle Vernon and/or North Belle Vernon were threatened from the areas along the river, Interstate 70 and/or the Belle Vernon Bridge.

Secondary Evacuation Zone: The Secondary Evacuation Zone is the area that the citizens of the Belle Vernon and North Belle Vernon Boroughs would be evacuated to in the event of a terrorist attack. The Secondary Evacuation Zone would be in effect if Belle Vernon and/or North Belle Vernon were threatened from the areas along the Central Business District and Rostraver Shopping Plaza.

Section A: In the case of the Primary Evacuation Zone: All citizens within Belle Vernon area in Fayette County would drive west on Route 906 onto State Street, continue up Broad Street toward Rostraver Shopping Plaza. Proceed to the vacant facility that once housed the Ames

Department Store. Overflow can proceed to the former SuperValu distribution center. All citizens in the North Belle Vernon area in Westmoreland County should also proceed to the same areas. All churches along the main roads can also be used for overflow. Doctor's offices can only be used for immediate medical attention.

Section B: In case of the Secondary Evacuation Zone: All citizens with the Belle Vernon area in Fayette County will proceed on Route 906 along the river in the churches and the Maccabee Industrial Inc. facility. If necessary some overflow can proceed to the municipal building and the Fire Department. All citizens in the North Belle Vernon area in Westmoreland County will proceed down Broad Street to State and onto Route 906 to the same evacuation points. As stated in Section A, other churches that are not affected can also be used for overflow, and Doctors offices are only to be used for immediate medical attention.

All vehicles must still comply with standard procedures unless otherwise told by safety officials.

All traffic trying to proceed in the other direction will not be permitted.

There will be no "cross town" traffic unless absolutely necessary.

You must drive by the designated routes or as directed by safety officials.

Only Emergency Response vehicles can proceed in any direction other than the ones given.

If you are close enough to walk, please do not drive. It will cut down on traffic.

If possible the Red Cross will be available to help in any way possible. If Mon Valley Hospital, in Charleroi is not accessible, the Jefferson Hospital on Route 51 will be the other alternative. UPMC McKeesport will also be an alternative.

Some safety concepts to keep in mind:

Know your buildings emergency procedures. They are critical to your safety!

Always remain calm in any emergency.

If an evacuation is ordered, use the pre-designed route for leaving the area or the Central Business District.

If you cannot use the pre-designed route, heed all safety instructions and follow the general flow of traffic.

Pre-plan with family members how each will get home in the event of an evacuation.

Plan and discuss secondary access numbers and meeting locations with family members in the event that you unable to contact each other using normal methods.

History of Belle Vernon

Forty miles south of the city of Pittsburgh lay Belle Vernon Borough, which is nestled on the east bank of the Monongahela River. Belle Vernon is one of the oldest communities along the Monongahela River. As originally plotted, in the 1800's, the town contained 360 lots. Some of them were in Westmoreland County, but most of Belle Vernon is actually in Fayette County.

Because of Belle Vernon's location, it as well as other small cities in the Mon Valley has been known for such businesses as lumbering, boating building and many forms of manufacturing take place. It is told that this area was once inhibited by Indians, wild animals filled the land, and fish where a common sight in the river. This all changed when settlers moved into this area in the late 1700's.

According to the history of Fayette and Westmorland Counties, a man known as Noah Speers drew up what we know as the very first comprehensive plan for Belle Vernon around 1813. Noah's father was reasonable for buying land in Monongahela, and expanding to where Belle Vernon rests today. The streets of Belle Vernon in the 1800's were as follows: Water, Main, Solomon, Wood, Market, First, Second, Third, and Fourth. The alleys were as follows: Long, Pleasant, Strawberry and Flint

The first sale of land that took place was on April 18, 1814 and was purchased for ten dollars. A man by the name of Thomas Ward, who was a carpenter, purchased the land and built a house there. This house is known occupied by James Lewis. As more and more people moved into Belle Vernon, so did more businesses. In 1833 Solomon Speers and Morgan Gaskill built the first steamboat to be constructed in Belle Vernon. Then Henry Speer put a ferry in place along the Monongahela River.

Belle Vernon flourished with more development and William Eberhard founded a glass-manufacturing industry in 1836. This glass manufacturing industry was one of the major and chief businesses in Belle Vernon. Manufacturing provided many jobs to residents at that time. As Belle Vernon developed due to manufacturing so did the town itself.

History of North Belle Vernon

North Belle Vernon celebrated its 128th year as a Borough in February. The town site was laid out in April 1872 but was not incorporated as a Borough until February 28, 1876. The founder was a farmer and a sand dealer by the name of Louis M. Speer. The first election was held in May 1876. W. R. Springer was our first Burgess, which is also known as a representative of a borough. Other council members chosen in 1876 were Peter Corwin, Thomas Hunt, John S. Henry, J.C. Hasson and Francis Keistler. Elected school directors were Thomas Hunt, William Jones, Francis Keistler, J.A. Piersoll, and John S. Henry. The first council meeting was on June 2, 1876 at which Henry was President; Hasson, Secretary; Hunt as Treasurer; and Peter Corwin, Street commissioner. The first Borough tax was 1 1/2 mills, levied on July 27, 1876.

Samuel Dougherty, a carpenter, is claimed to have built the first dwelling in the new Borough on Broad Avenue. He was a very influential person in North Belle Vernon and served in the offices of Justice of the Peace, Council Member, School Director, and Judge of Election, all at the same time. His carpenter shop was also the temporary school. The first two industries in the town were a Foundry in 1873 on Broad Avenue above and a Flour Mill on Speer Street in 1874. Lots were not sold until 1900 and this is when the area really started to build up. The population was 435 in 1890 and by 1910 it grew to 1520. The 1960 census showed 3,184 residents, followed by 2,916 in 1970, 2,245 in 1980, and 2,112 in 1990, and the most recent count in 2000 was 2,107.

North Belle Vernon has a very good business base with an estimated figure of approximately 100 retailers. We have moderate business base of approximately one hundred merchants.

North Belle Vernon is one town that can boast of one of the most modern fire departments with the latest equipment, all of which was purchased by funds raised by the department. The fire department celebrated its 100th anniversary in 1995. Police Chief James D. Bedsworth heads the present force of eight officers who provide twenty-four hour protection to North Belle Vernon. The borough is currently trying to replace all the sanitary sewers.

Along with the modern Fire Department, North Belle Vernon's library is also a facility that is supported and maintained by the residents. The residents take pride in the fact they are willing to keep things moving in their small but progressive town. Public school children attend classes at Belle Vernon Area School District sites located in adjacent Washington and Rostraver Townships. Our one private school, Saint Sebastian, currently has 250 students from preschool to grade eight.

Current Conditions in Belle Vernon:

Route 88 is a heavily traveled roadway in the Mid Mon Valley region. This roadway may have the potential to become a major commercial road and there is still some development along the road even though there are the other major interstates in the area.

The North Belle Vernon area is also trying to come up with a new economic strategy. Any economic strategy should address the following elements:

. Identifying sites needing improved infrastructure and access;

Identifying opportunities and developing recommendations for retrofitting,

Buildings and sites to current standards

Conducting an analysis of vacant space with strategies on how to market the

Space to progressive, but complimentary firms,

. Suggesting standards for lighting, signage and streetscape improvements that will create a
   unified visual appeal for new development,

. Defining the obstacles that are located in this central business district, which

Might hinder business growth (i.e. zoning, lack of infrastructure),

. Identifying traffic and parking issues,

. Determining what types of public investment are needed to assist in this process,

. Identifying the issues that could be of concern to local business owners such as public safety,
   lack of space, lack of a business organization, perceptions, community identity and
   proper mix of business types.

Economic Development

The Washington County Council on Economic Development is a private non-profit
located in Washington, PA, the county seat. This organization offers technical assistance,
financing and education to businesses located in Washington, Greene, Fayette and Westmoreland
Counties. The Mon Valley Progress Council is located in Monessen, Westmoreland County that
has the goal to revitalize the economy of the Mid Monongahela Valley through industrial
development. The Mon Valley Progress Council has been a leader in supporting the development
and construction of the Mon Fayette Expressway.

A workforce development strategy must be created that addresses what types of industries / businesses are needed to support the region in the future. Public policies must then be implemented that will support the development strategy and work to bring about economic growth.

One goal of the economic development strategy should be to establish industry business clusters within the Mid Mon Valley Region. The objective of an industry is to support local businesses and increase the economic vitality of the region. Often industry strategies are implemented to solve crises such as high unemployment rates, recession, stagnant economy, real estate collapse, or loss of key industries. An industry is an interconnected group of firms and industries within a region that conduct business with one another and or share a common need for talent, technology, and infrastructure. The firms and industries may be competitive with other members in the cluster and or they may cooperate with other members.

The Mid Mon Valley Planning and Zoning Commission and local elected officials should initiate networking efforts and planning sessions; ensuring economic development is undertaken through a regional approach. Steps should be taken to open communication and foster relationships with existing business and industry leaders, California University of Pennsylvania, Mon Valley Regional Chamber of Commerce, and Washington County Chamber of Commerce and other local chambers or economic development organizations. Sustainable development is an important issue where businesses and elected officials must consider their relationship and obligation to the community or region in which they are located. These officials should take into consideration the economic, environmental, and social sustainability of their development efforts. Businesses in the region today will need to focus on minimizing the wasteful use of their resources, along with equity and community well being. A strong regional approach to economic development will be essential and a well thought out zoning ordinance can achieve land use goals to foster and support economic growth.

Business Located in Belle Vernon

Kelly's Car Wash

California Boat Club

Morgovich Signs

Darby's

Roscoe Ledger

Spee-D Mart & Sunoco Gas Station

Justine's Personal Care Home

Furniture Restoration

White Barn Restaurant

Trisha's Paws & Claws

Johnny's Market

Uptown Saloon

Walker Landscaping

Lagerheads

Adult Assisted Living

Kim T's Ball

Busters R & R Builders

Rotheram Plumbing, Heating, and Cooling

Kelly Incorporated

Garret Insurance Agency

Highway Appliance

Flo's Personal Home Care

Loskos Auto

Fox's Pizza

Mon Valley Community Credit Union

CMM Associates

Storage Building

Route 88 Auto Sales

Creative Designs & Expressions

Melenyzer Funeral Homes Inc.

Hardhat Saloon

Auto Repair

Braun's Bakery Outlet

Patricia Roberts Hair Salon

Roscoe Laundry

C.L. Electronics

Jay's Tavern

J & J Transmissions

Charlie Roberts Auto Repair

Central Apartments

Bradish's Marina

Dunlevy Diving Center

Cadillac Joes

McIntosh Masonry & Excavating

Mariner's Hall Dentist Office

Stile Investments & Tax Professionals

Zanardini Water Service

Bonn Paralegal and Tax Service

Rosko's Bar

Union Cleaners

D & S Variety

Caul's Garage

Annette's Beauty Salon

Cupari Home Improvement

Churches in Belle Vernon

ANTIOCH BAPTIST CHURCH, 412-929-3044

942 HENRY STREET, BELLE VERNON PA 15012

FIRST BAPTIST CHURCH, 412-929-6968

511 SHORT STREET, BELLE VERNON PA 15012

OLIVE BRANCH BAPTIST CHURCH, 412-929-2466

RURAL ROUTE 3, BELLE VERNON PA 15012

SALEM BAPTIST CHURCH, 412-379-7702

RURAL ROUTE 4, BELLE VERNON PA 15012

PEOPLES BIBLE CHURCH, 412-929-5402

1101 HENRY STREET, BELLE VERNON PA 15012

SAINT SEBASTIAN'S CHURCH, 412-929-9300

801 BROAD AVENUE, BELLE VERNON PA 15012

COVENANT CHRISTIAN CHURCH, 412-929-9373

36 MAIN STREET, BELLE VERNON PA 15012

FIRST CHRISTIAN CHURCH, 412-929-2441

320 MAIN STREET, BELLE VERNON PA 15012

LYNNWOOD LUTHERAN CHURCH, 412-929-4760

900 WASHINGTON ROAD, BELLE VERNON PA 15012

FELLS UNITED METHODIST CHURCH, 412-379-4502
RURAL ROUTE 1, BELLE VERNON PA 15012

FIRST UNITED METHODIST CHURCH, 412-929-4696
200 STATE STREET, BELLE VERNON PA 15012

CHURCH OF THE NAZARENE, 412-929-7196
112 REED AVENUE, BELLE VERNON PA 15012

FIRST PRESBYTERIAN CHURCH, 412-929-7616
501 FAYETTE AVENUE, BELLE VERNON PA 15012

MARION PRESBYTERIAN CHURCH, 412-929-7380
207 PERRY AVENUE, BELLE VERNON PA 15012

REHOBOTH PRESBYTERIAN CHURCH, 412-929-7020
RURAL ROUTE 3, BELLE VERNON PA 15012

Hospitals & Airports

Hospitals/medical centers near Belle Vernon:

MONONGAHELA VALLEY HOSPITAL INC (about 7 miles; MONONGAHELA, PA)

BROWNSVILLE GENERAL HOSPITAL (about 8 miles; BROWNSVILLE, PA)

UPMC MCKEESPORT HOSPITAL (about 15 miles; MCKEESPORT, PA)

Airports certified for carrier operations nearest to Belle Vernon:

   ALLEGHENY COUNTY (about 16 miles; PITTSBURGH, PA; ID: AGC)

   ARNOLD PALMER REGIONAL (about 34 miles; LATROBE, PA; ID: LBE)

   MORGANTOWN MUNI-WALTER L. BILL HART FLD (about 34 miles;
      MORGANTOWN, WV; ID: MGW)

Other public-use airports nearest to Belle Vernon:

   ROSTRAVER (about 7 miles; MONONGAHELA, PA; ID: FWQ)

   FINLEYVILLE AIRPARK (about 12 miles; FINLEYVILLE, PA; ID: G05)

   BANDEL (about 15 miles; EIGHTY FOUR, PA; ID: 22D)

Colleges/Universities, Public/Private Schools, & Library

Colleges/Universities with over 2000 students nearest to Belle Vernon:

CALIFORNIA UNIVERSITY OF PENNSYLVANIA (about 5 miles; CALIFORNIA, PA; Full-time enrollment: 5,183)

WESTMORELAND COUNTY COMMUNITY COLLEGE (about 22 miles; YOUNGWOOD, PA; FT enrollment: 3,223)

CARNEGIE MELLON UNIVERSITY (about 23 miles; PITTSBURGH, PA; FT enrollment: 7,903)

ART INSTITUTE PITTSBURGH (about 24 miles; PITTSBURGH, PA; FT enrollment: 2,246)

POINT PARK COLLEGE (about 24 miles; PITTSBURGH, PA; FT enrollment: 2,189)

UNIVERSITY OF PITTSBURGH-MAIN CAMPUS (about 24 miles; PITTSBURGH, PA; FT enrollment: 22,930)

DUQUESNE UNIVERSITY (about 24 miles; PITTSBURGH, PA; FT enrollment: 8,199)

Public high school in Belle Vernon

BELLE VERNON AREA HS (Students: 910; Grades: 09 - 12)

Public primary/middle schools in Belle Vernon

ROSTRAVER ELEMENTARY SCHOOL (Students: 671; Grades: KG - 05)

MARION EL SCHOOL (Students: 668; Grades: KG - 05)

BELLMAR MS (Students: 377; Grades: 06 - 08)

ROSTRAVER MS (Students: 350; Grades: 06 - 08)

Private primary/middle school in Belle Vernon

ST. SEBASTIAN'S SCHOOL (Students: 239; Location: 815 BROAD AV; Grades: PRE-K - 8)

Library in Belle Vernon

BELLE VERNON PUBLIC LIBRARY (Operating income: $42,721; Location: 505 SPEER ST; 21,339 books; 110 audio materials; 229 video materials; 17 serial subscriptions)

Radio & Television Stations

Strongest AM radio stations in Belle Vernon

WASP (1130 AM; daytime; 5 kW; BROWNSVILLE, PA; Owner: KEYMARKET LICENSES, LLC)

WFGI (940 AM; 0 kW; CHARLEROI, PA; Owner: KEYMARKET LICENSES, LLC)

KDKA (1020 AM; 50 kW; PITTSBURGH, PA; Owner: INFINITY BROADCASTING

OPERATIONS, INC.)

WWNL (1080 AM; 50 kW; PITTSBURGH, PA; Owner: STEEL CITY RADIO, INC.)

WKHB (620 AM; 6 kW; IRWIN, PA; Owner: BROADCAST COMMUNICATIONS, INC.)

WPTT (1360 AM; 5 kW; MCKEESPORT, PA; Owner: RENDA BROADCASTING
CORPORATION OF NEVADA)

WWCS (540 AM; 5 kW; CANONSBURG, PA; Owner: BIRACH BROADCASTING
CORPORATION)

WJAS (1320 AM; 6 kW; PITTSBURGH, PA; Owner: RENDA BROADCASTING CORP.
OF NEVADA)

WEAE (1250 AM; 5 kW; PITTSBURGH, PA; Owner: ABC, INC.)

WPIT (730 AM; 5 kW; PITTSBURGH, PA; Owner: PENNSYLVANIA MEDIA
ASSOCIATES, INC.)

WWVA (1170 AM; 53 kW; WHEELING, WV; Owner: CAPSTAR TX LIMITED
PARTNERSHIP)

WBGG (970 AM; 5 kW; PITTSBURGH, PA; Owner: AM/FM RADIO LICENSES, L.L.C.)

WPGR (1510 AM; 5 kW; MONROEVILLE, PA; Owner: MCL/ MCM- INC.)

Strongest FM radio stations in Belle Vernon

WOGI (98.3 FM; DUQUESNE, PA; Owner: KEYMARKET LICENSES, LLC)

WOGG (94.9 FM; OLIVER, PA; Owner: KEYMARKET LICENSES, LLC)

WVCS (91.9 FM; CALIFORNIA, PA; Owner: FOREVER OF SOMERSET, INC.)

WVPM (90.9 FM; MORGANTOWN, WV; Owner: WEST VIRGINIA EDUCATIONAL BROADCASTING AUTHORITY)

WSHH (99.7 FM; PITTSBURGH, PA; Owner: RENDA B/CING CORP. OF NEVADA)

WZPT (100.7 FM; NEW KENSINGTON, PA; Owner: INFINITY RADIO SUBSIDIARY OPERATIONS INC.)

WRIJ (106.9 FM; MASONTOWN, PA; Owner: HE'S ALIVE INC.)

WDSY-FM (107.9 FM; PITTSBURGH, PA; Owner: INFINITY RADIO SUBSIDIARY OPERATIONS INC.)

WJJJ (104.7 FM; PITTSBURGH, PA; Owner: CAPSTAR TX LIMITED PARTNERSHIP)

WWSW-FM (94.5 FM; PITTSBURGH, PA; Owner: AM/FM RADIO LICENSES, L.L.C.)

WLTJ (92.9 FM; PITTSBURGH, PA; Owner: WPNT, INC.)

WLSW (103.9 FM; SCOTTDALE, PA; Owner: L. STANLEY WALL)

WQED-FM (89.3 FM; PITTSBURGH, PA; Owner: WQED MULTIMEDIA)

WDVE (102.5 FM; PITTSBURGH, PA; Owner: CAPSTAR TX LIMITED PARTNERSHIP)

WKST-FM (96.1 FM; PITTSBURGH, PA; Owner: CAPSTAR TX LIMITED PARTNERSHIP)

WRRK (96.9 FM; BRADDOCK, PA; Owner: WPNT INC)

WSSZ (107.1 FM; GREENSBURG, PA; Owner: MCL/MCM-INC.)

WANB-FM (103.1 FM; WAYNESBURG, PA; Owner: BROADCAST
COMMUNICATIONS, INC.)

WBZZ (93.7 FM; PITTSBURGH, PA; Owner: INFINITY RADIO SUBSIDIARY
OPERATIONS INC.)

WDUQ (90.5 FM; PITTSBURGH, PA; Owner: DUQUESNE UNIVERSITY)

TV broadcast stations around Belle Vernon

W26AV (Channel 26; CHARLEROI, PA; Owner: DEBRA GOODWORTH)

WPCB-TV (Channel 40; GREENSBURG, PA; Owner: CORNERSTONE TELEVISION,
INC.)

WQEX (Channel 16; PITTSBURGH, PA; Owner: WQED MULTIMEDIA)

W65CG (Channel 65; PITTSBURGH, PA; Owner: TRINITY BROADCASTING
NETWORK)

WPXI (Channel 11; PITTSBURGH, PA; Owner: WPXI-TV HOLDINGS, INC.)

WTAE-TV (Channel 4; PITTSBURGH, PA; Owner: WTAE HEARST-ARGYLE TV, INC.
(CA CORP.))

WPTG-LP (Channel 69; PITTSBURGH, PA; Owner: ABACUS TELEVISION)

WBGN-LP (Channel 59; PITTSBURGH, PA; Owner: BRUNO GOODWORTH
NETWORK, INC.)

WCWB (Channel 22; PITTSBURGH, PA; Owner: WCWB LICENSEE, LLC)

KDKA-TV (Channel 2; PITTSBURGH, PA; Owner: CBS BROADCASTING INC.)

34

WPGH-TV (Channel 53; PITTSBURGH, PA; Owner: WPGH LICENSEE, LLC)

WQED (Channel 13; PITTSBURGH, PA; Owner: WQED MULTIMEDIA)

WBPA-LP (Channel 29; PITTSBURGH, PA; Owner: VENTURE TECHNOLOGIES
GROUP, LLC)

W61CC (Channel 61; PITTSBURGH, PA; Owner: THE VIDEOHOUSE, INC.)

WIIC-LP (Channel 29; PITTSBURGH, PA; Owner: ABACUS TELEVISION)

W63AU (Channel 63; PITTSBURGH, PA; Owner: THE BON-TELE NETWORK, INC.)

WBYD-CA (Channel 35; JOHNSTOWN, PA; Owner: BENJAMIN PEREZ)

WNPB-TV (Channel 24; MORGANTOWN, WV; Owner: WEST VIRGINIA
EDUCATIONAL BROADCASTING AUTHORITY)

Housing

Houses: 720 (612 occupied: 349 owner occupied, 263 renter occupied)

Rooms in owner-occupied houses in Belle Vernon, Pennsylvania:

1 room: 0

2 rooms: 0

3 rooms: 0

4 rooms: 29

5 rooms: 72

6 rooms: 104

7 rooms: 58

8 rooms: 10

9 or more rooms: 76

Rooms in renter-occupied housing units and apartments:

1 room: 9

2 rooms: 28

3 rooms: 93

4 rooms: 56

5 rooms: 62

6 rooms: 5

7 rooms: 0

8 rooms: 10

9 or more rooms: 0

Year house built:

1999 to March 2000: 35

1995 to 1998: 19

1990 to 1994: 16

1980 to 1989: 9

1970 to 1979: 101

1960 to 1969: 5

1950 to 1959: 64

1940 to 1949: 117

1939 or earlier: 354

Bedrooms in owner-occupied houses in Belle Vernon:

No bedroom: 0

1 bedrooms: 0

2 bedrooms: 110

3 bedrooms: 166

4 bedrooms: 65

5 or more bedrooms: 8

Bedrooms in renter-occupied apartments and housing units:

No bedroom: 9

1 bedrooms: 130

2 bedrooms: 92

3 bedrooms: 32

4 bedrooms: 0

5 or more bedrooms: 0

Household type by relationship

Households: 1177

In family households: 851 (217 male householders, 74 female householders)

225 spouses, 277 children (259 natural, 0 adopted, 18 stepchildren), 24 grandchildren, 17 brothers or sisters, 17 parents, 0 other relatives, 0 non-relatives

In non-family households: 326 (85 male householders (72 living alone)), (217 female householders (198 living alone)), 24 non-relatives

In group quarters: 14 (0 institutionalized population)

Size of family households: 146 2-persons, 66 3-persons, 51 4-persons, 13 5-persons, 7 6-persons, 8 7-or-more-persons

Size of non-family households: 270 1-person, 32 2-persons, 0 3-persons, 0 4-persons, 0 5-persons, 0 6-persons, 0 7-or-more-persons

Role of the Professional Planner

When developing an Evacuation plan for the area of Belle Vernon our group as taken on the role of professional planners. The following is a list of the information and the stages that will need to be followed.

Gather background data

Analyze and interpret the data

Communicate that data to the planning body and public

Organize and present information to the proper authority

Compile information and feedback from the presentation

Develop alternative plans

Develop appropriate plans, policy, and producers.

Plan accessible and coherent documents to the proper authority or public.

Put in to place.

Information on the Professional Planner comes from:

Becker, B & Kelley, E. (2000). Community Planning: An Introduction to the

Comprehensive Plan. Island Press, Washington D.C.

Washington Co. Redevelopment Authority, 2002-2003, Washington Chamber of Commerce, 2002

Chapter 2

Urban Planning of Somerset County

Introduction

This project will give you an overview of ubran plan of the overall area of Somerset County through history of employment, economic development, annual income, census, places of interest for economic purposes. This project will include statistics in charts, graphs and maps to give a better idea of what Somerset County in comparison with the state of Pennsylvania have for their economic purposes. There will be problems of the economy in this region that will have a solution.

History of Somerset County

Well before the time of ancestry, there were three Indian tribes in Somerset County that were the Shawnee, Iroquois and Delaware along the Southern Trail. This trail later would be call Route 40. During this time, there was also a northern trail called Forbes Road. Forbes Road was later changed to Route 30. There first city and township to ever be found in this area was Quemahoning Township with the city named Kickenapauling's Town.

http://www.somersetcntypachamber.org/galleries/history/history-1.HTM

By the early 1700's, this was not a populated area anymore and not disturbed. The

area was referred as "an old abandoned village". This early site in this region was carbon dated in 980 A.D. by the Monongahela Woodland Culture.

http://www.somersetcntypachamber.org/galleries/history/history-1.HTM

The Europeans was the first people in this area to hunt and trap. There were two men named Isacc Cox and Harmond Husband completely against the British government system. In 1869, they formed a group called the Regulators to fight against unfair taxes and fees. However, despite outnumbering the British soldiers; the British had better weapons and more ammunition. For these reasons, Husband and his fighting crew had to retreat.

http://www.somersetcntypachamber.org/galleries/history/history-1.HTM

In 1783, the town of Hannastown was destroyed. As soon as Husband heard of this, he wanted to move his precious family to Fort Cumberland for more of security blanket from Indian attacks. In 1784, Husband, Peter Ankeny and Ulrich Bruner made out plans for the town of Millfordtown. This town by people, who knew Bruner, called it "the town that Bruner laid out or

Brunerstown. http://www.somersetcntypachamber.org/galleries/history/history-1.HTM

During the Whiskey Rebellion era, (1790's) whiskey and grain was the value of business in this area. At first, there was no tax on whiskey for tavern owners to buy it or even sell it. Later on, the Congress would pass a bill because American government needed the money, so this was an idea to gain more of a profit towards building and developing the local community areas. For this reason, the people in Western Pennsylvania would rebel against the tax. This gave President Washington no choice in the early 1790's but to enforce the tax. It was witnessed that despite the 13,000 soldiers to upheld the new past tax law that Husband and General Robert Philson of Berlin, Pennsylvania would represent their protest to building a liberty pole. They and others was arrested and tried but never convicted in a Philadelphia courtroom for their protests of this controversial tax. http://www.somersetcntypachamber.org/galleries/history/history-1.HTM

In 1795, the County of Somerset was formed from the town of Bedford. The community and area of Somerset County elected its first official, which was Alexander Addison. The past urban planning and development of Somerset county consisted of county jail of logs and soon to be courthouse. During the different eras of the three courthouses, the first court house lasted from 1801-1852 and was built of stone. The second courthouse consisted of brick, cupola, and two stories tall from 1853-1904. The final court house of which is standing today is much larger of the other two buildings. As the population and census increased, so did the need for a much larger building in 1907 as it is today.
http://www.somersetcntypachamber.org/galleries/history/history-1.HTM

In 1804, Somerset became the first to be named a Borough. There would be three devastated fires that would happen to these citizens beloved town. The first one was in 1833 in which the first started from Edgewood Avenue and Diamond. The total damage of this past urban development was 80,000 dollars including: six stables, nine businesses, and ten ships total. Nearly forty years later in 1872, the second fire caused this small community was ninety buildings and 300,000 dollars worth of damage. The final devastating fire was in 1876 in which it started at the stables of Somerset Foundry and moved eastward destroying homes, hotels and stores. http://www.somersetcntypachamber.org/galleries/history/history-1.HTM

Over the next forty years, the inventions and responsibilities would be even greater through electricity, light, water, and sewage. These technologies made the urban planning and development much easier because people in their communities had pipes running through their houses and homes instead of getting it through wells and rivers near by. Some houses had their own lighting through light bulbs. In 1879, William Gilbert was responsible for lighting lamps for a dollar a day, but not for no more for seventeen days out of each month. However, for any certain reason if there was an extra day or more he was needed then he would get paid the extra dollar per day. This was only available five days a week. There would not be any twenty-four hours and seven days a week until 1914. In the early 1890's, several companies were developed in the Somerset County area to make the Somerset area more business like and attract new people to their building town. These companies were the Somerset Phone Company, Somerset Water Works Company, Somerset Phone Company and

volunteer fire department. http://www.somersetcntypachamber.org/galleries/history/history-1.HTM

The excitement of past citizens and planners of Somerset County from the village of Somerset of the early 1800's to the town size population development 1900's see a great growth and economic development through the great ideas and strides from our founding fathers. From our founding fathers to today as Somerset County residents, we must build the best community and urban plan possible to make the small area of Somerset better.

http://www.somersetcntypachamber.org/galleries/history/history-1.HTM

Local Areas and Attractions of Somerset County

Kooser State Park Family Cabin District was built for the purpose of future camping development. This area was very significant for several purpose of the camp development which are: conservation, social history, architecture, landscape, entertainment, recreation, and politics. This state park is on the right side or eastern side of Mount Davis. This is also the location of where thousands and thousands of acres was destroyed by the May 31st and June 2nd Salisbury Tornadoes. This is about 8 miles away from Salisbury and 10 miles away from Rockwood. The period of significance was 1925-1949. This was added in 1987.

http://www.nationalregisterofhistoricplaces.com/PA/Somerset/state.html

Mount Davis is the highest point in Pennsylvania located in Southwestern Somerset County at 3,213 feet in elevation. The reasons why so many people are attracted to this area of Somerset County are hiking, walking, running, picnic out, see deer and bear once in awhile. This location also has a 100 foot tower to view two different states: West Virginia, and Maryland elevations range from 2500 to 3100 feet.

http://www.nationalregisterofhistoricplaces.com/PA/Somerset/state.html

High Point Lake is a body of water about 15 minutes away from Mount Davis, Koosier State Park and Confluence. This area of attraction is from locals to fish and swim. This body of water flows into the Youghigeny River. High Point Lake Walleyed fish, Bass, Pike, and Catfish. http://www.nationalregisterofhistoricplaces.com/PA/Somerset/state.html

The Youghigeny River is a big time river for fishing and the time for swimming especially in June through September. The Youghegeny River flows into the Monogehela River in the Pittsburgh area. The River has been above flood stages in the Confluence area in January of 1996 at 29.0 feet which is about 2 feet above sea level. This caused schools and roads to be closed for several days. http://www.nationalregisterofhistoricplaces.com/PA/Somerset/state.html

The Laurel Hill State Park is located about 10 minutes away from Seven Springs Mountain Resort. The Laurel Hill State Park was built for out of staters to camp, fish and swim and enjoy the summer time in the beautiful area of Somerset County. The time period of which this place was significance was 1925-1949. This was an addition in 1987 to the National Register of Historical Places. http://www.nationalregisterofhistoricplaces.com/PA/Somerset/state.html

The Petersburg Tollhouse was added to the County's National Register of Historical Places in 1979. This area of importance is located off of U.S. 40 in Addision about 8-10 miles away from Confluence. The main importance of this location was transportation and road related situations. This is a museum in which the period of significance is from 1825-1849. http://www.nationalregisterofhistoricplaces.com/PA/Somerset/state.html

The Somerset County Courthouse was added to the National Register of Historical Places in 1980. The courthouse system in this community has been around for 200 years. The main importance is for local government and law purposes. This is where court decisions have been decided for years. The period of time of significance is 1900-1924.

http://www.nationalregisterofhistoricplaces.com/PA/Somerset/state.html

All the related bridges of the Somerset County area from 1800-1949 were significant for one reason from the stagecoach era to the automobile era was transportation or to get a crossed one place to another. These places are: Barronvale Bridge, Beechdale Bridge, Jenner Township, Glessner Bridge, King's Bridge, Lower Humbert Bridge, New Baltimore Bridge, Shaffer's Bridge, Trotstletown Bridge, and Walter Mill's Bridge. These areas of Somerset County which they are located in Rockwood, Confluence, Somerset, Boswell, Stoystown, and Windber. These bridges of the Somerset county area and community were added to the National Register of Historical places in 1980.

http://www.nationalregisterofhistoricplaces.com/PA/Somerset/state.html

The following historical districts from 1991-2002 are: Windber, uptown Somerset twice, Stoystown, and Boswell. All of these districts were added through the different years above from the National Register officials of the local Somerset County area These different historical areas of Somerset County have period of significance from 1800-1949. The areas of significances are architecture, community planning and development, social history, industry, and historical- non aboriginal. http://www.nationalregisterofhistoricplaces.com/PA/Somerset/state.html

On September 11th, 2001, we will never forget what happened in Shanksville, Pennsylvania. The Flight 93 crew and passengers will always be remembered for the day they risked their own lives to stop the Terrorists from taking over the plane. This is why there is a Flight 93 Memorial that will be forever lived as forty ordinary people changed the era for all time to come. These heroes prayed for strength, relief, faith and common courtesy for them uniting as one to stop at devastating terrorist attack. These people deserve all are gratitude for such bravery and courage! http://www.flt93memorialchapel.org/

New Businesses added

The Confluence House Bed & Breakfast and Catering Services, LLC

A Victorian style home, built in the early 1900's and located in the heart of Confluence. The Confluence House offers four guest bedrooms on the second floor and a spacious three room suite on the top floor. Rooms have queen beds, three private baths, air conditioning and most importantly, comfort. Relax on the front porch swing. Safely store your bicycles and gear in our locked garage. http://theconfluencehouse.com

The Garrett Bed and Breakfast is a place for tourists to stay and enjoy local activities in Somerset County. This Victorian Queen Anne is one of the oldest homes located in Garrett, Pennsylvania. It was built in 1903 and is owned and operated by the seventh generation of the family Wanda Broadwater. It has spacious and luxurious rooms with a crowning touch turret necessary for a queen. Start your mornings with a delicious country homemade breakfast or a breakfast to go. We want your stay to be an enjoyable one and hope you'll experience unmatched comfort and convenience. http://www.garretthousebb.webs.com/

The Garrett House is the ideal location for your Somerset County and surrounding area plans. It is situated within a few blocks and easy access to the Bike Trail. It is centrally located for the following recreational areas:

- The Great Allegheny Passage
- Windmill Farm
- Seven Springs, Hidden Valley and The Wisp Resorts
- Nemacolin Woodland
- **White Water Rafting** (Ohiopyle, Savage/Yough Rivers)
- Piney Run Golf Course
- Flight 93 Memorial / **9 Miners**
- Falling Water
- Kentucky Knob
- Yough and Cheat Rivers
- French and Indian War Sites
- Pennsylvania Maple and Autumn Glory Festivals
- Rails to Trails
- Hunting, Fishing, Camping, Hot Air Ballooning
- Somerset **and** Garrett **County Fairs**
- Mountain Playhouse
- Frostburg State University
- **Amish Country**

http://www.garretthousebb.webs.com/

Urban Development of Somerset County of Transportation and Activities

The Somerset County residents would like to see more hiking trails and biking trails just like the specialized areas of Forbes State Forest and Laurel Highland hiking trails. There is a bike route that has not been developed, but this route is supposed to run from Pittsburgh to Washington D.C. The part of Somerset county has been completed by August 2001 and its 29 half miles long from Meyersdale to Confluence. The rest of the project from Confluence to McKeesport was 71 miles long and was finished a couple of years later.

http://www.somersetcntypachamber.org/scripts/chamber/site/AdventureSports.cfm

There are trips at a value of 200 bucks for interested Somerset county people. This route now completed is total at 300 miles. This is an eight day trip and will bring more entertainment and more bikes through the Somerset county area. The estimated total cost for this adventurous trip would be 950 dollars with 20 people together. This trip will prove of how effective this trail will be for urban business as well. Will people actually want to move to an area like Somerset County because of just an Allegheny Highland Trail, if you're a hiker, exerciser then this is the place for you! Somerset County will always be a quiet area with farming, cows, runners, walkers, hikers, bikers and of course snowy winters. http://www.atatril.org/yoktrek/2004trek.htm

There are other sports in Somerset county people enjoy, such as whitewater rafting, hunting and fishing. The deer hunting in late November through middle of December is big for county residents because they are always looking for snow to make tracking deer easier. People can enjoy whitewater rafting at Ohio Pyle. The hunters are glad for the three state game lands of Gallitzin, Forbes State Forest, and Laurel Hill State Park. These areas hunters can thrive on during the different seasons of the year with variety of animals depending on the season. http://www.nationalregisterofhistoricplaces.com/PA/Somerset/state.html

There are also areas for fishing for local Somerset County residents. These areas for citizens are Cranberry Glade Lake, High Point Lake, Lake Somerset, Laurel Hill Lake, and Quemahoning Reservoir. The location of Cranberry Glade Lake is about 8 miles South of Confluence Route 3003. High Point Lake is 342 acres long and wide. Lake Somerset is a half a mile away off of Route 219 in Somerset. The specific area and location of Laurel Hill Lake is Laurel Hill State Park right off of Route 31 near Trent. The Youghiogheny River is located along

Somerset and Fayette County line in the Confluence area. This river is 2,800 acres long and wide. http://www.nationalregisterofhistoricplaces.com/PA/Somerset/state.html

Enviromapper analysis of Somerset County

This map I printed out shows the different wastes and pollutants that danger the environment of Somerset County from the United States Environmental Protection Agency. There are several wastes and pollutants: water dischargers, superfund, hazardous waste, toxic releases, emissions and BRS. These waste and pollutants affect the following areas: Somerset, Friedens, Berlin, Meyersdale, and Rockwood. The most affected area is Somerset because of harmful toxic wastes and BRS from the most populated community in the county itself with the most business too. So, cars will cause smoke and so will well going businesses like food industries, factories, manufacturer companies. The coal mine areas of Meyersdale, Berlin and Boswell have trouble with hazardous waste and releases through cars, buildings and polluted rivers like the Casselman and Youghiogheny River.

http://maps.epa.gov/scripts/.esrimap?name=enviroMapperN&Cmd=NavPan&CmdOld=ZO

County Elected Officials of Somerset County Ideas

The different elected county officials of today are: James Marker- Chairman and Commissioner, Brad Cober- Commissioner, Pamela Tokar-Ickes Commissioner, Jerry Spangler-District Attorney's Office, Wallace Miller-County Coroner, Carl Brown- County Sheriff, Donna Matsko Schmitt -County Treasurer, Shelley Glessener- County Auditor, Linda Jo Berkey-County Register of Wills, Patricia Brant- County Recorder of Deeds, and Mary Dinning- Clerk of Courts. These county elected officials have hopeful plans for Somerset County, such as better urban planning by building more businesses, and attractions. Projects from these elected officials are to clear polluted water from the Casselman River of Meyersdale to Youghiogheny River of Confluence for better fishing and swimming conditions and to drink as well. There has been a recent electrical cleaner project in the Garrett, Somerset and Meyersdale area for the need for windmills in 2000. There are seven windmills in Garrett, ten in Meyersdale and ten more in Somerset for a more non pollutant protective environment.

http://www.naco.org/Template.cfm?Section=Find_a_County&Template=/cffiles/counties

Somerset County of Planning Facts

Population Percentages

The population of Somerset County was 79,553 people while the whole state of Pennsylvania 12,287,150 people. Population percent change was -0.6% while there was no change at all in PA. The population in 2001 in the county of Somerset was 80,023 people while PA had 12,281,054 people. The population percentage change from 1990-2000 was 2.3 percent increase while in PA 3.4 percent increase. Somerset County is at a 5.2% in comparison to PA at 5.9%. Somerset County is at 22.3% in comparison to PA at 23.8%. The elderly of 65 years or older in Somerset County population percent in 2000 is 18.0% to PA's 15.6%. The percentage population of females in Somerset County in 2000 is 50.1% to PA's 51.7%. The white people population percent of Somerset County in 2000 is at 97.4% to PA's 85.4%. Black or African Americans population percent in Somerset County in the year 2000 is 1.6% to PA's 10.0%. This data is supported by chart A. http://quickfacts.census.gov/qfd/states/42/42111.html

Education/Working Travel

People living in the same house in 1995 and 2000 population percentage of ages five and above is 70.6% in Somerset County and PA's at 63.5%. The foreign born person in the year 2000 for population percentage in Somerset County is 0.7% in comparison with Pa's at 4.1%. The population percentage of High school graduates from 25 years and older in 2000 is 77.5% for Somerset County and 81.9 for PA. The Bachelor degree population percentage in 2000 in Somerset County is 10.8% and 22.4% in PA. The mean travel time to work in Somerset County is 22.5 minutes to the state wide average of 25.2 minutes. This data is supported by chart B. http://quickfacts.census.gov/qfd/states/42/42111.html

Housing/Income

The housing units in 2000 in Somerset County are 37,163 to PA's 5,249,750. The homeownership rate for 2000 in Somerset County is 78.1% to PA's 71.3%. Somerset County is 11.9% to PA's 21.2%. The owner occupied housing units for the median value in 2000 in Somerset County is $70,200 to $97,000 in PA. Somerset County is 31,222 to PA's 4,777,000. The person per household in 2000 for Somerset County is 2.45 to PA's 2.48. The household income for median purposes in 1999 for Somerset County is

30,911 and $40,106 for PA. The Per Capita money income in 1999 for Somerset County is $15,178 and $20,880 for PA. The data is shown by charts C-F

http://quickfacts.census.gov/qfd/states/42/42111.html

55

Employment/Sales

The Private nonfarm establishments in 1999 for Somerset County are 21,173 and 4,986,591 for PA. The percent change of nonfarm employment from 1990-1999 for Somerset County is 8.9% and 8.4% for PA. The non employer establishments in 1999 for Somerset County is 4,309 and 614,594 for PA. In 1997, the manufacturers shipments in Somerset County is 644,063 to Pa's 172,193, 216.The retail sales in 1997 for Somerset County is 543,075 to 109, 948, 462 for PA. The full-time equivalent and local government employment is 2,015 for Somerset County to Pa's 365,550. This data is supported by Chart G-I.

http://quickfacts.census.gov/qfd/states/42/42111.html

Location Facts of Somerset County to Pennsylvania

The land area in 2000 in square miles in Somerset County is 1,075 to PA's 44,817. The persons that owned per square mile is 74.5 in Somerset County to 274.0 in

PA. This data is supported by chart J-L below.

http://quickfacts.census.gov/qfd/states/42/42111.html

Conclusion

Somerset County in comparison with the state of Pennsylvania the population statistics have dropped slightly since the 1990's. The problem to this is getting solved with good Somerset County planner and citizen ideas by cleaning up the environment and attracting businesses to the beautiful quiet country area through great local government ideas as well.

Chapter 3

Oklahoma City NBA Expansion Stadium Project

Introduction

In expanding the National Basketball Association to Oklahoma City there are major factors that have to be taken into account. These factors include getting a background on professional sports expansion in order to get a clear view of how successful a team will be in the expanded area. Other factors are positioning the facility to house them so that it can be a recreational and cultural incentive to that area. The expansion site within a walking distance to other attractions would prove to be beneficial because it could possibly be a magnet for spectators within the Oklahoma City area. Also, drawing economically stable businesses to the area as well. This paper will give a literature review of various past expansion ventures that occurred throughout the country to confirm the potential site for the sporting facility, and give a brief explanation of why the site was selected.

Literature Review of Sports Stadiums

Our literature review consisted of eight articles. We focused on past expansion sites, their success and failures, research studies on profitability of new stadiums and the "honeymoon period". It is through this literature review that we have substantiated our decision for placing a NBA stadium slightly north of downtown Oklahoma City.

Below we have listed the articles we reviewed along with an article summary and opinion.

An Empirical Review of the Stadium Novelty Effect

Howard, Dennis & Crompton, John (2003). Sports Marketing Quarterly. Volume 12, Number 2:111-117, 2003

Summary

This article is to be an empirical review of two questions. The first question to ask is. Is there proof that a "novelty effect" happens when new stadiums are opened? The second question is. Who investigates if the franchises have better attendance with the new facility than without? Through research, they have discovered that 45% of all major league sports have constructed a new facility since 1995. Of these teams, the average attendance increase was 22.2%. However, they did note a decrease in each year following the opening season. This evidence supports the first question that there is a honeymoon period. Now to the important question most business people want to know. Is the team better off with the new stadium? The answer is yes. Evidence showed that even though there were drastic decreases in attendance each year after the initial season. 9 out of 10 teams for which comparisons could be made showed appreciable gains in attendance over totals reported in the years preceding their moves to new facilities.

Opinion

This article was good for our research because it proved that a new facility has a positive effect on attracting viewers. Also, it has hard data to back up its findings. Another positive point is this article stated that NBA teams had the best increase in attendance related to a new arena.

NFL Teams Profiting From New Venues, By: Morell, John, Amusement Business, 00032344, 05/21/2001, Vol. 113, Issue 20

Summary

A case between the NFL and the Raiders shed some light on financial balance sheets that the league has kept private. These balance sheets were shocking to confirm what we all thought. Teams with newer stadiums out ranked the other teams in operating profits. It concluded that the increased revenue streams that new stadiums bring are extremely lucrative. The article sited the Cleveland browns as an example. The Browns were last in the league for performance, but first in profits. It was stated that in 1999 they had an operating profit of $36.5 million. They were also first income from parking and advertising. As a result, the Cleveland Browns brought in $22 million. The glamour of these increased profits must not be taken out of context. A new expansion team and gain from a new facility does come with a price. The franchise fee for the Cleveland Browns to the NFL was $476 million. So, you truly do need money to make money.

Opinion

I agreed with the article that new stadiums do increase the revenues for the teams. I learned that there are a lot of expenses that come with a new team that I may not have thought of before. This article helps us in planning our expansion site because of the real life examples with the Cleveland Browns.

Are Public Policies Needed To Level The Playing Field Between Cities and Teams?

Rosentraub, Mark S. (1999)   Journal of Urban Affairs; Dec99, Vol. 21 Issue 4, p377, 19p

Summary

The NBA sports market forces a lifestyle for stadiums in suburban life in national transportation and housing programs. This also affects the imperatives of global competition followed by many leaders to think about how they must have attractive ideas to attract teams to the capitals of the states. (Kantor and David 1988) They concluded by saying "The structure of markets had created a highly dependent position for cities."

All Communities can refuse to meet certain needs. The cities in some cases have most certainly dropped the issue for bidding wars and firms, when the costs become too high. (Hudnut 1993; Nunn & Schoedel, 1995).

The modern era of practice has provided many financial opportunities, but the most popular is subsidies. These are supposed to have attracted different teams after the 1953 season of sports. Baltimore was anxious to bring a MLB team; making the following attractions available by funding a second deck on Municipal Stadium and benefits of a loan to save the St. Louis Browns from going bankrupt made this possible. In 1954, the St. Louis Browns franchise was desperate to get out of town because of so many losing seasons. They decided Baltimore was a profitable area because of the attraction (Morgan, 1997). The year of 1956, Los Angeles wanted a franchise, so the Brooklyn Dodgers were persuading by several attractions, which included land, and other incentives. These incentives in persuasion for selection of specific locations were the choice of the owners. These incentives were ranged from tax abatements and expenditures for infrastructure to the people to buy luxury suites and unsold tickets. The professional sports teams now play their respective sports in public funded ballparks, stadiums and arena. These teams do not need to be responsible for its facility's capital and operational needs (Noll Zimbalist, 1997).

The NBA selects certain locations and areas for a new expansion team by also deciding how the revenues and players will be equally distributed between different market sizes and values. The communities not selected or advised to hold a team by the NBA will have to put more effort to satisfy their community. The result will be no possibility for an expansion team.

The biggest one of the investments for a ballpark was in Denver by Federico Pena, the mayor who brought MLB to Denver. This was quite important to the mayor as he quoted "I think if you're going to compete in the global marketplace you've got to step up to the plate, so to speak, in many areas, and one is you have to have a major sports teams in your city" (Whitford, 1993, p. 30). In 1997, the state of Indiana declared its matter of public reason to build a new arena for the Pacers which the legislature supported a tax supported plan of 109 million dollars for the new arena. Another example is in the NFL, when Indianapolis financed the Colts through the idea to convert tax dollars to the project of renting cars to finance the team.

Opinion

In my opinion, this idea to create attraction to big cities with the money and smaller communities is a big disadvantage. The bigger cities have much more attraction with much more spending money. Some communities or cities have a budget to follow by and some do not. So, some cities cannot step up to the plate of opportunity to bring in a major league team. This is why it is a disadvantage.

Cities, Sports, and Economic Change: A Retrospective Assessment

Rosentraub, M.S. (2002) Journal of Urban Affairs; Dec2002, Vol. 24 Issue 5, p549, 15p

Summary

The fact that sports, tourism and entertainment are for recreational inventions or to undertake leadership is not very surprising. The cities involved have been central places of commerce, culture and cutting edge occurring projects. The focus on urban renewal was developed because of the idea that center cities were flooded with criminals. The previous thought was different from recent thoughts of designing pictures of the cities and to make urban centers more attractive, such as diversity, tourism, culture, and commerce. That was the old focus, but the modern focus is involving trial and error in response to everyday economic changes and conditions within policy leading advising that resulted in equality between business and entertainment strategy. The period of the 1970's through the 1990's saw nearly all central cities; big suburban and other communities target their goals on downtown economy efforts on the hospitality industry. This trend would lead to the building of sports facilities all over the United States for all professional sports as a goal for the past 30 years. The smaller cities that are behind the modern sports facilities built in the modern age look on at Baltimore, Cleveland, Dallas, Denver, Indianapolis, and Phoenix have now made their goals towards minor league teams. The cities that have professional sports facilities show they let this economic development carry the load for the city's financial spending. Then, they tried to redevelop the strategy by giving up some space and area for a stadium for minor league teams. But, despite this fact, there are independent case studies in numerous facts that teams and structures surrounding it is not related with any city's economic development. Working together on several issues for any city has been about building facilities for all professional sports teams (Rosentraub, 1999, 2000). In the idea, these sports facilities can bring back the historical background between business, recreation, tourism, and downtown areas (Newman 2002).

Opinion

In my opinion, over the last 30 years these coming attractions to downtown areas, such as arenas, stadiums and ballparks will be the future of all sports and profit. The coming attractions may sometimes work out or may not work out. This is why the higher city officials hope or assume the money and profiting will come in.

Tourism, Sports and the Centrality of Cities

Turner, R.S., Rosentraub, M.S. Journal of Urban Affairs; Dec2002, Vol. 24 Issue 5,

p487, 6p

Summary

The focus of incorporating the downtown area in the 1970's and 1980's was to build an effort for a corporate organization. The purpose of public sector resources was to reverse the falling property values (Frieden & Sagalyn, 1990). The businesses focused its goal on its interest

in bringing retail activity back to the downtown to get more attractions to the stadiums in

downtown areas.

Commercial real estate rose to the occasion in the early 1990's. However, the festival

market places failed to produce positive answers. The cities started to turn to new forms of

financial opportunity by supplying more tourist attractions, such as stadiums, arenas and parks.

The cities would also turn to sports for the main attraction. The first major recent sports park to

bring major attraction to downtown areas was the stadium that Baltimore built for the Orioles at

Camden Yards This stadium definitely brought a pastime tradition to bring people to the ballpark

through tourism, culture and entertainment. However, hockey and basketball weren't far behind

as downtown areas tried to bring as much consumption of money as possible to their area. This

was not always successful. As a result, city officials thought for sure it would bring more

population, money, and immigrants to these areas. The city's hope was a positive central city

economic activity. One example is when people didn't want a team in Seattle. However, the

Seattle baseball team was still approved without any real results because of the money not

materializing like it should have. The theory of the business people of St Petersburg, Florida was

to build a venue without any sports team and assume a team would bid on their area. However,

this was not the case either to enhance their financial profits. This bidding, however, would have

been a bad move for St. Petersburg because many cities got bad financial deals. The downtown

sports corporations were enthused by purchasing the naming rights to ballparks and stadiums.

These newer sports facilities were used to attract higher financial standards and select a certain audience through their advertisements.

Opinion

In my opinion, the downtown areas, such as St. Petersburg, Seattle and Baltimore shows experiences of success and failure of persuading teams into their respective towns. This shows that cities are never guaranteed to get sports teams to their area no matter what they do through economic matters.

The Impact of Stadiums and Professional Sports on Metropolitan Area Development

Baade, Robert A. Growth and Change, spring 1990, Vol 21 Issue 2, pl, 14p, 4

Summary

The debate about proponents of subsidization; it's a matter of planning the responsibility. In laymen terms, the responsibility of having a stadium exceeds its economic budget. The economic effort comes from all kinds of sources. These economic producing solutions are rent, concessions parking, advertising suite rental and other preferred seating rental. However, direct expenses come from income wages, related expenses, utilities, repairs, maintenance, insurance policies and debt. Benjamin Oker (1974)

In the metropolitan areas, the rent pays the sports team's attendance. Let's give you an example, for instance, the Chicago Whitesox have signed a lease for twenty years. In the lease, it states The Chicago Whitesox will pay their landlord, (Illinois Sports Facilities Authority or known as ISFA) for every seat sold 2.50 each 1.2 to 2 million and 1.50 with 2 million excess.

This is for the first ten years of this lease, but the second ten years of the contract is a bit more expense because there is more to be paid off. Every seat sold $4.00 per ticket goes to the ISFA in excess to 1.5 million to 2 million sold and 2 million or more for 1.50 each ticket to ISFA. If this not the case that none of the expectations are reached then ISFA must purchase 300,000 tickets, if only the attendance is not met at 1.5 million. The Whitesox have a successful year in drawing at least 1.2 million people in the last 10 years of the lease. Then, the ISFA will pay the Whitesox 1 million per year. (State of Illinois 1988) In the Whitesox history have never drawn over 2 million respectively, but only in 1987 and 1988 have they ever drawn over 1.1 million per year.

Opinion

In my opinion, when two higher businesses go out it to satisfy each other it's always a battle to win the war. I would never take the Chicago Whitesox to own or to finance a new stadium with because there has not been enough people coming over to see their games in a 50-year history and until this is proven then people will not come to the ballpark.

The Employment Effect of Teams and Sports Facilities

Baade, Robert A., Sanderson, Allen R., Sports, Jobs and Taxes: the economic impact of sports teams and stadiums; Washington, D.C. Brookings Institution Press 1997

Summary

This article focuses on the negligible increase in spending and new jobs. The types of jobs sports subsidies generate the cost of creating jobs through these subsidies.

The spots facilities do bring in new jobs, while hurting the businesses that have already been in the area. The article also mentions that money earned by coaches, players etc. goes mainly into the national market, not local. The money earned may not necessarily benefit that area directly. Also, sports facilities that are built in areas where there is not a saturated sports market can prove to be economically beneficial as well. Jobs created by these new facilities are considered "trade" and "service" employment. These make up 98% of jobs creates by these sports facilities. Since, these jobs are created by seasonal sports; they are part-time, which means this type of employment does not prove to be as beneficial as one might think. In addition to having these jobs created; they are often supported by having taxpayers sometimes pay hundreds of thousands of dollars in order to support these positions.

Opinion

As a taxpayer, I am appalled that my money goes toward something I have absolutely no interest in. There are bigger issues that need to be approached such as helping the sick and homeless. These facilities also run a high risk of hurting businesses that have already been in the area for some time. Take for instance, small family owned businesses in the area; they may not survive after such changes are made. The "Powers that Be" would not really take this into consideration because it's not their mother's bakery or their uncle's convenience store that will be suffering.

Stadiums and Urban Space

Rosentraub, Mark S., Sports, Jobs and Taxes: the economic impact of sports teams and stadiums;

Washington, D.C. Brookings Institution Press 1997

Summary

Sporting facilities surrounded by acres of parking lots have different set of interaction than a facility within walking distance of restaurants, Office complexes, and other recreational facilities. This article states that recently people are more likely to migrate towards the suburbs. It goes on to say that when people shop, they have totally different feelings that are aroused than that from being at a sporting event. The two actions require separate types of energies to be evoked. Of the two cities studied, the results prove that population in those central business districts declined as well as job opportunities when sporting facilities were brought into the area. One of the cities managed to slow the suburbanization process by having a sporting facility that hosted many events of amateur teams that came from outside areas. When it comes to building sporting facilities to slow this decentralization process down those in charge of the project should proceed with caution because disappointed in this area occurs more often then not.

Opinion

I think people try to come up with quick fixes to issues that affect their cities instead of looking at deeper issues that may in turn prove to be beneficial. Maybe that area could use a new shopping mall or lower taxes. There could be several reasons why those who live in central cities choose to relocate to suburbanized areas. Sporting facilities may seem to work for a short period of time, but eventually things will be the same or maybe worse. Building these facilities in troubled cities can be compared to a bandage. Bandages do not help wounds to heal; they only cover them up.

In conclusion, this literature review did help us decide where to place our stadium. We gained knowledge about the benefits of locating near restaurants and other attractions. Our group learned the importance of planning the financial cost of constructing. Also, the future economic impact of the stadium is with all possible parties to be involved. Through this literature review, we studied other cities successes and failures. We will be taking from their experiences to help make our project the most successful.

Strengths of this area for expansion

Oklahoma City has many strengths. Their first strength is that they're 45th in the TV viewing market and have a population of 3,258,100. Secondly, Oklahoma City was ranked 2nd lowest for cost of doing business in the nation. Also, Oklahoma University is nearby and has developed a region of loyal sports fans. Finally, the city itself has many other tourist/leisure attractions. Here is a list of some of the local attractions: Remington Park Race Track, National Sports Hall of Fame, Lincoln Park, Forest Park, Edwards Park, Kirkpatrick Center, State Capital, Oklahoma Historical Society, Oklahoma City University, Oklahoma Art Center, and National Cowboy Hall of Fame Western Heritage Center.

We've decided the stadium will be built along two heavily traveled interstates I-35 and I-44. The reasoning for this location is its proximity to local attractions and the availability of land. Remington Park Race Track and The National Cowboy Hall of Fame Western Heritage Center are two of the closest attractions.

73

Set up for new stadium

We began to make our base map with the data given to us. This included shape files such as Oklahoma City itself and a landmark polygon theme. These attractions include larger areas such as shopping centers, airports, and lakes. A landmark point theme shows landmarks such as a high school and a cemetery. Finally, the road shape file makes up of all the roads in Oklahoma City.

First, we changed the color of each theme in order to make it easier to distinguish between them. Second, we used the Identify Tool to identify the interstates. Third, we made them easy to locate with the addition of interstate symbols to the map. We also added graphics to the map indicating the hospital, the airport, and the Air Force base.

The first shape file we created on our map highlights the three interstates that run through the downtown area of the city includes I-35, I-44, and I-235. The next shape file we created indicates a half-mile buffer around the three interstates. This shape file is important because it aids us in placing the stadium approximately a half-mile from the interstate, and insures us that the exit ramp will be approximately a half-mile in length.

The next step we took in the making of our map involved geocoding addresses of some of the most popular attractions Oklahoma City has to offer. By using the Measure Distance tool, we can affirm that the geocoded attractions range from about one to four miles in distance from the stadium.

The last two shape files that were added to the map indicate the stadium itself and the exit ramp leading from Interstate-44 to the stadium. Using the draw tool to locate a rectangle on the outer edge of the half-mile interstate buffer created the stadium. The rectangle was drawn carefully by first changing the distance units to feet under the View Properties menu in order to ensure that the stadium was drawn in a proper stadium size. Our stadium turns out to be approximately 821,000 square feet in size.

There are five maps included in the Attached Maps section of this paper. Each one portrays the steps taken in selecting and verifying the site for the new stadium.

Conclusion

We concluded that this was the best possible site for our stadium in Oklahoma City because of the sporting attractions that include the National Sports Hall of Fame, Remington Park Race Track, and the National Cowboy Hall of Fame, etc. Our facility would also be within walking distance to shopping venues, Parks, and other interesting attractions. These along with other components should be enough to attract new businesses and create new jobs as well. Although, there is no definite way to insure a team's success with a new sporting attraction in this area, however, the odds are in our favor.

Chapter 4

Allegheny and Washington County Planning Studies

<u>I.) Problem defined: hypotheses, assumptions and theories</u>

The problems with the region of western Pennsylvania are in the Washington and Allegheny counties that the results are lack of jobs, lack of income, population decreasing and a real sense of financial security. The reason for all of these problems is because the government puts more time into other things such as: cutting salaries for people, who have worked for a long time, laid off long time workers, and do not give the workers of Pennsylvania enough benefits. There are several reasons why the part of western Pennsylvania in general is struggling with the economic development. The problems include the steel mills are gone from the early 1900's from which the brilliant Andrew Carnegie built in the early 20th century to boost the economy. As a result, thereafter workers would be out of jobs by the

1970's and 1980's from Donora to Pittsburgh. In this area, thousands of jobs would be lost because of no money being put toward the steel mills and bankruptcy would follow. There will have to be a need for more of every job just like there is in professional and clinical jobs in the near future.

II.) Overview of Allegheny and Washington counties

Whiskey Rebellion

The late 1700's saw a revolt against an excise tax on whiskey in 1791 that angered many American citizens. This was in the areas of Western Pennsylvania including: Washington and Allegheny counties. The results of this tax were to no satisfaction of the farmers as there would be no real business for selling or any importance of cash crop. The settlers would file disputes against the Federal Government for this reason.

http://www.earlyamerica.com/earlyamerica/milestones/whiskey/

The people in the Washington and Allegheny county regions were not accepting this tax well at all. There would be riots everywhere until the tax was lifted or lessened. The insurrection really opened itself to violence when tax collectors were attacked all the time. In July of 1794, several hundred men rebelled against an inspector by torching his home, barn and several buildings surrounding his home.

http://www.earlyamerica.com/earlyamerica/milestones/whiskey/

In Pittsburgh at the time, there was outrage there as well. So, on August 7th 1794, the President at the time, George Washington, had no choice, but to enforce the military under the 1792 Militia Law by protecting the union to make sure everything would be okay. The president's order was to set up at least 13,000 troops. This action resulted in the first official defense against rebellions in United States history. There were several arrests and they got out of jail after Washington pardoned them in Philadelphia.

http://www.earlyamerica.com/earlyamerica/milestones/whiskey/

National Road

George Washington and General Braddock originally founded the National Road in the mid 1750's. This road was used for military purpose. However, Thomas Jefferson thought of the idea to open the road further to extend travel to greater distances after buying the Louisiana

78

Purchase for economic growth and development. However, this road would not be completed to Wheeling until 1818. This road would extend as far as Vandlia, Indiana in the 1830's, but with no funds the construction was stopped. The National Road opened the Ohio River Valley for settlement and good economic development. http://www.nps.gov/fone/natlroad.htm

The first years of the road being completed attracted frequent travelers to the west of the Allegheny mountain. In this region, there was rich and fertile land to be settled upon by in the Ohio River Valley Region. This road's growth was also responsible for the increase in population. There were several cities along the National Road that was affected, which was Cumberland, Uniontown, Brownsville, Washington, and Wheeling. This road had economic growth by developing taverns, blacksmith shops and livery stables for travelers that went through small towns and villages. The main reason for this was so travelers and tourists had somewhere to go to make them business or to stay the night. http://www.nps.gov/fone/natlroad.htm

The taverns were by far the best business for the National Road because it was referred as the modern "truck stop". There were two kinds of these taverns, the expensive tavern was known as Stagecoach Tavern and the other tavern everyone could afford was the Wagon Stand. This tavern offered three different services, such as food, drink and lodging.
http://www.nps.gov/fone/natlroad.htm

The traffic would be outrageous during the day and early evening hours just like the Baltimore Beltway is today. The stagecoaches usually traveled for 60 to 70 miles per day. There was another type of transportation that only traveled 15 miles per day, which was the Conestoga wagon. This wagon was referred as the 19th Century "tractor trailer". The Conestoga was developed to carry heavy weight west over the Allegheny Mountains. This design of this wagon looked like brightly painted with red running gears and also Prussian blue bodies and white canvas coverings. http://www.nps.gov/fone/natlroad.htm

After 1850, the railroad industry started to take business away from the National Road and all was doomed from the start as all businesses especially taverns went out of business. The railroad was strongly not encouraged in the Pittsburgh area for the reason stated above. However, the railroad would proceed into Pittsburgh by 1852. The B & O Railroad destination reached as far as Wheeling in the same year. http://www.nps.gov/fone/natlroad.htm

In November1879, Harper's Magazine quoted "The national turnpike that led over the Alleghenies from the East to the West is a glory departed... Octogenarians who participated in the traffic will tell an inquirer that never before were there such landlords, such taverns, such dinners, such whiskey... or such an endless cavalcades of coaches and wagons." An unnamed poet quoted " We hear no more the clanging hoof and the stagecoach rattling by, for the steam king rules the traveled world, and the Old Pike is left to die."
http://www.nps.gov/fone/natlroad.htm

A new period of time began with the invention of the automobile in the early 20th century by Henry Ford. The National Road was revived after also being almost dead business wise because of the lack of travelers and businesses going bankrupt. However, the automobile would revive the National Road from a dirt road to a nice smooth paved road with business attractions replaced by the old taverns and other old business attractions with motels, hotels, restaurants and service stations to build the business what it would be today. However, some if not most of the traffic was deverted away because of two happenings the Federal Highway Act of 1921 and

Federal Act of 1956 created a highway system of roads for Pennsylvania and other states as well.

http://www.nps.gov/fone/natlroad.htm

Summary

The unemployment rating for Washington was slightly higher than Allegheny's from 5.9

to 5.7 in 2003. However, employment versus unemployment stats shows from 1996 to 1999 that

employment was on the rise with unemployment down from 57.2 percent in 1996 to 50.1 percent

in 1999. The table from the Pennsylvania economic development book shows a raise of 12 to15

dollars per year from 1059.00, 1074.00, 1090.00 and finally 1,102.00. (2000- Pennsylvania

Abstract Book)

According to the Pennsylvania economic development book, the jobs for whites outnumber

blacks easily. In the region of Washington county and Allegheny county, the jobs for the white

are higher for males from 190,167 to the females at 174,760. However, for the employment for

the blacks, the female is out number from 19,070 to 14,365. The most popular position for whites

in the Pittsburgh region is professionals. The most popular position for blacks in the Pittsburgh

region is sales workers. (2000-Pennsylvania Abstract Book)

The population and income for 1999 between Washington and Allegheny is much higher

because of the city of Pittsburgh and its 1 million populations but slow job decline and

population projections show this to be true. These future population projections show from 2000-

2015 that an average of 30,000 to 45,000 people will leave the Pittsburgh and Allegheny by the

81

year 2015. http://www.palmids.state.pa.us/INCOME.asp?geo,

http://www.palmids.state.pa.us/POPULAT.asp?geo

The population in 2000 was 1,265,184, but by 2015 will be 1,157001. The employment

projection according to the U.S. Bureau of Labor Statistics in November 2001 will need more

jobs for physician assistant services will increase 53 percent by 2010. Also, the job profession is

one of the top 15 growing jobs people go to for a living. According to a National PA

Demographics fact, there was a per capita distribution of 8.83 per 100 K population ranks 32 out

of 50 states. http://pittsburgh.bizjournals.com/pittsburgh/stories/2003/08/25/daily12.html

The average person would make about 7,000 dollars more near Pittsburgh than in

Washington, PA. There are about 1 million people more in Allegheny than in Washington. These

results show the economy is dying because of the population projection drops slightly every five

years. Despite, the late 1990's surge for income and wage improvement when Governor Rendell

in the early 21st century, he took over, it was all downhill from there. (2000- Pennsylvania

Abstract Book)

The average weekly earnings went slightly up each year from 1997 to 1999. The average

weekly hours dropped slightly from 43 to 42.5 from 1997 to 1999. The average hourly earnings

show a slight rise from 14.71 to 15.3 by 1999. Allegheny County has the advantage for money

coming and dominates every economic type of job, such as services by 10 million dollars,

manufacturing by 4 million, government enterprises by 2.5 million, and about 2,500 more dollars

in farming than Washington as well. (2000- Pennsylvania Abstract Book) For additional information, these charts below will provide all data of employment from Washington County and Allegheny areas.

Conclusion

In Conclusion, the economic development stats show slight rises in wages, income and whites working more than blacks in the late 1990's. However, since Rendell has taken over Washington and Allegheny counties have unemployment rates of 5.9 percent to 5.7 percent. The population projects show that the economic interest in this area and state of Pennsylvania will drop unless there will be more tourist attractions. Statistics will have to show in the near future in favor of every kind of job possible just like in the professional fields and clinical fields, but we must have a better leader than Rendell or all hope will be lost.

Chapter 5

Natural Resource Conservation District

Chapter 6

Shade Creek Watershed Project

References

An Empirical Review of the Stadium Novelty Effect

Howard, Dennis & Crompton, John (2003). Sports Marketing Quarterly. Volume 12, Number 2:111-117, 2003

NFL Teams Profiting from New Venues, By: Morell, John, Amusement Business, 00032344, 05/21/2001, Vol. 113, Issue 20

Oklahoma City Convention and Visitors Bureau Website

Are Public Policies Needed To Level the Playing Field between Cities and Teams

Rosentraub, Mark S. (1999) Journal of Urban Affairs; Dec99, Vol. 21 Issue 4, p377,19p

Cities, Sports, and Economic Change: A Retrospective Assessment

Rosentraub, M.S. (2002) Journal of Urban Affairs; Dec2002, Vol. 24 Issue 5, p549, 15p

Tourism, Sports and the Centrality of Cities

Turner, R.S., Rosertraub, M.S. Journal of Urban Affairs; Dec2002, Vol. 24 Issue 5,

p487, 6p

The Impact of Stadiums and Professional Sports on Metropolitan

Baade, Robert A. Growth and Change, Spring 1990, Vol 21 Issue 2, pl, 14p, 4

Stadiums and Urban Space

Rosentraub, Mark S., Sports, Jobs and Taxes: the economic impact of sports teams and stadiums; Washington, D.C. Brookings Institution Press 1997

The Employment Effect of Teams and Sports Facilities

Baade, Robert A., Sanderson, Allen R., Sports, Jobs and Taxes: the economic impact of sports teams and stadiums; Washington, D.C. Brookings Institution Press 1997

The National Road- Fort Necessity NB, March 28, 2003,

http://www.nps.gov/fone/natlroad.htm

Milestone Historic Document – The Whiskey Rebellion

http://www.earlyamerica.com/earlyamerica/milestones/whiskey/

2000 Pennsylvania Abstract, 2000

Preliminary Population Projections, 1990,

http://pasdc.hbg.psu.edu/pasdc/Data_&_Information/Data/228a.html

University of Texas Southwestern Medical Center at Dallas, 2003,

http://www8.utsouthwestern.edu/utsw/cda/debt48950/files/54147.html

Pennsylvania Labor Market Information Database System, 2000,

http://www.palmids.state.pa.us/INCOME.asp?geo

Pennsylvania Labor Market Information Database System, 2000,

http://www.palmids.state.pa.us/POPULAT.asp?geo

Pittsburgh Business Times, August 28, 2003,

http://pittsburgh.bizjournals.com/pittsburgh/stories/2003/08/25/daily12.html

www.ingramcontent.com/pod-product-compliance
Lightning Source LLC
Chambersburg PA
CBHW032103280526
45784CB00013B/3004